THIS BOOK BELONGS TO

....

First published in Great Britain in 2024 by Hodder & Stoughton
An Hachette UK company

1

A CIP catalogue record for this title is available from the British Library

Hardback ISBN 978 1 399 81942 8
eBook ISBN 978 1 399 81943 5

Page design by Isobel Gillan isobel@isobelgillan.co.uk

Printed and bound in China by Leo Paper Products Ltd

Hodder & Stoughton policy is to use papers that are natural, renewable and recyclable products and made from wood grown in sustainable forests. The logging and manufacturing processes are expected to conform to the environmental regulations of the country of origin.

Hodder & Stoughton Ltd
Carmelite House
50 Victoria Embankment

The authorised representative in the EEA is
Hachette Ireland, 8 Castlecourt Centre, Dublin 15,
D15 XTP3, Ireland (email: info@hbgi.ie)

THE LORD'S PRAYER

A Beginner's Guide

STEPHEN COTTRELL

Illustrated by Jack Seymour

THE LORD'S PRAYER is the most famous prayer in the world.

It is said in just about every church service, from the coronation of the King to the christening of a newborn child.

It is the first prayer many people ever learn. It is probably the last one most people say.

At the last count, it has been translated into 1,437 languages.

It is the prayer Jesus taught his friends. That's why we call it THE LORD'S PRAYER. It is the prayer the Lord Jesus gives us.

First of all, just twelve people knew it – the twelve disciples Jesus gathered around him. Today, it is said by millions of people across the world.

If you know THE LORD'S PRAYER already, then this is a book to help you understand what it means.

If you don't know the prayer, this book will encourage you to learn it by heart and say it each day.

THE LORD'S PRAYER comes from the heart of God to our hearts.

It is a challenging prayer. It teaches us how to pray. But it also teaches us how to live.

It is an invitation to live differently – to live the way Jesus shows us.

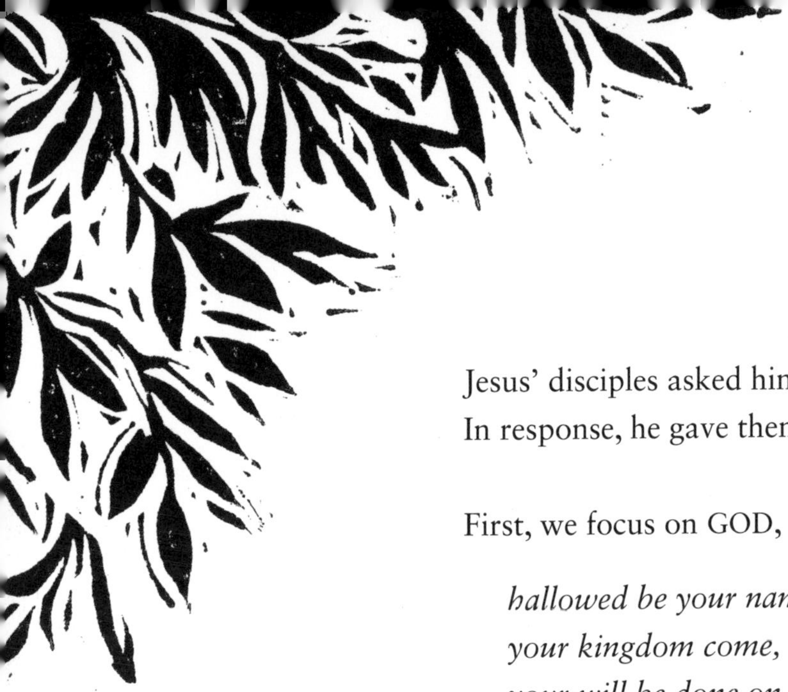

Jesus' disciples asked him to teach them how to pray. In response, he gave them this prayer.

First, we focus on GOD, who is our FATHER:

hallowed be your name,
your kingdom come,
your will be done on earth as in heaven,

And then we focus on our NEEDS:

Give us today our daily bread
Forgive us and help us to forgive others
Lead us not into temptation and deliver us from evil.

In fewer than seventy words, Jesus gives us a prayer to learn by heart and a prayer to get inside our hearts, shaping the way we live.

In THE LORD'S PRAYER, we offer our thanks and our concerns to God. But this prayer teaches us something too. It is teaching us what we should want, what we need, what we should ask for and how we should behave. It is training our hearts.

THE LORD'S PRAYER comes from the heart of God, *via* Jesus to our hearts, and *through us* to all the world, so that we can all pray 'thy kingdom come on earth as it is in heaven'.

There are two slightly different versions of THE LORD'S PRAYER used in churches in England:

Our Father in heaven,
hallowed be your name,
your kingdom come,
your will be done,
on earth as in heaven.
Give us today our daily bread.
Forgive us our sins
as we forgive those who sin against us.
Lead us not into temptation
but deliver us from evil.
For the kingdom, the power,
and the glory are yours
now and for ever.
AMEN.

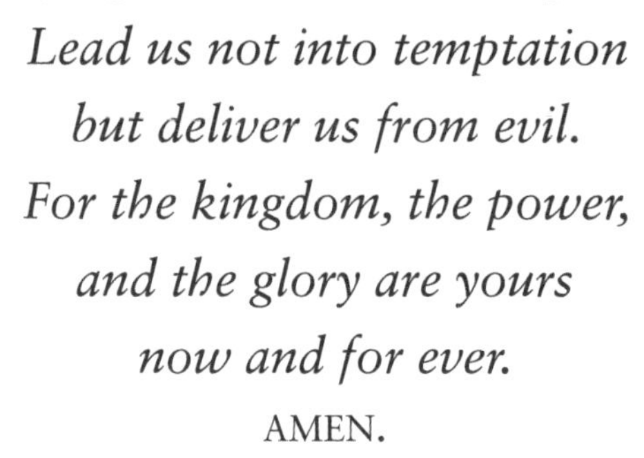

Our Father, who art in heaven,
hallowed be thy name;
thy kingdom come;
thy will be done;
on earth as it is in heaven.
Give us this day our daily bread.
And forgive us our trespasses,
as we forgive those who trespass against us.
And lead us not into temptation;
but deliver us from evil.
For thine is the kingdom,
the power, and the glory,
for ever and ever.
AMEN.

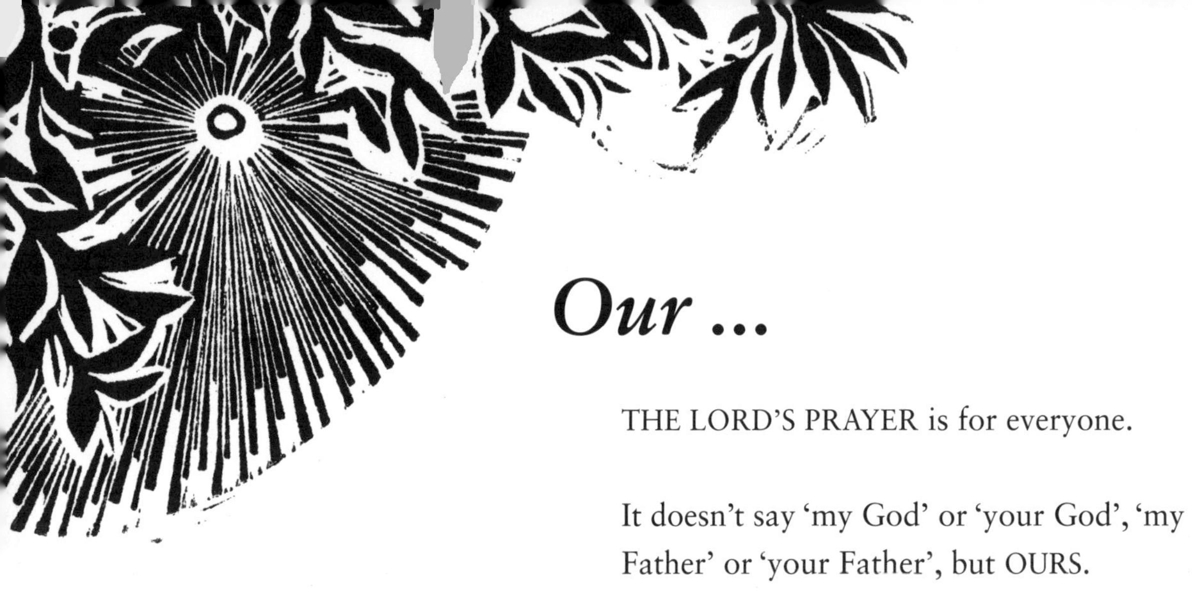

Our ...

THE LORD'S PRAYER is for everyone.

It doesn't say 'my God' or 'your God', 'my Father' or 'your Father', but OURS.

Together, we are the household of God, a worldwide family, a huge network of women and men, boys and girls.

EVERYONE is counted in.

When we say this prayer, we are saying that everyone else who says it is our sister and brother.

Father ...

Jesus called God his dad.

The actual word Jesus used was Abba, which is a word like Daddy.

Not all families have a father. Some people have had a bad experience of fathers and mothers.

God is there for us. Jesus teaches us that God is a loving Father. That even if our parents sometimes let us down, God will never let us down.

When we say this prayer, we
come to God like a child coming
to a loving parent and receiving
a great big hug
We are known.
We are loved.

Who art in heaven ...

Think of heaven as a 'WHAT' rather than just a 'WHERE'. What is heaven? It is *being completely with God*.

To be in heaven is to live with God as a loving Father, and with Jesus as our brother. We are welcomed into the community of God.

Heaven also begins now. It begins when we become part of the Church, the household of God.

It continues beyond this life, where we will enjoy life with God for ever.

When we say this prayer, we come closer to that 'with God' promise of heaven.

Hallowed
be thy
name

God's name is hallowed, or HOLY.

The word 'holy' means the 'most special', or the 'most beautiful'. God's name is so special and beautiful you can't measure it!

Because God is the Creator, the one who made everything, then everything that is good and beautiful comes from God. God is the source and beginning of everything.

God exists outside of the universe. But in Jesus, God has come into the world to show us the beautiful holiness of God and to help us live our lives with God.

When we say this prayer,
we remember just how very special
and very beautiful God is.

Thy kingdom come

This kingdom of God is wherever and whenever God is King.

Jesus often spoke about the kingdom of God. Almost the first thing he says in the Bible is that the kingdom is near. 'Repent,' he says, 'and believe this good news.'

'The kingdom is near' means it is available. It is a new way of living that we can enter into now.

'Repent' means that we need to turn around. We are going in the wrong direction. We need to follow Jesus and let him teach us how to live.

The good news is that when we enter the kingdom, we live a new way, following the way of God that Jesus shows us.

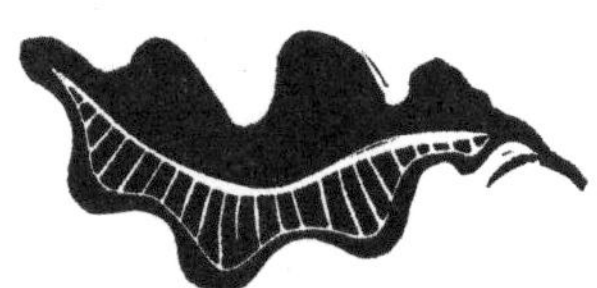

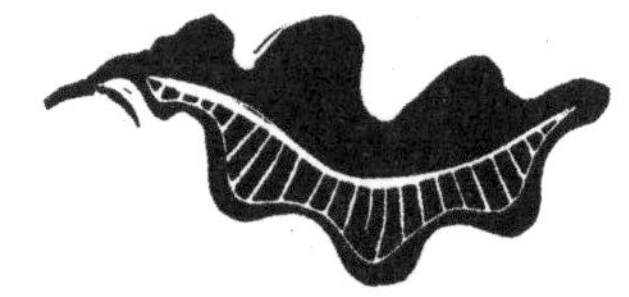

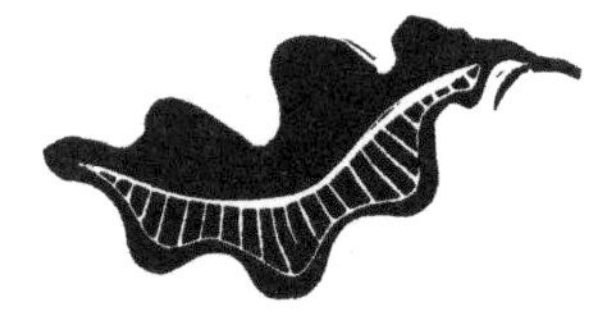

Jesus said that the kingdom of God is like a mustard seed. It is the smallest of all the seeds, yet it grows into a huge tree.

The kingdom of God can also start small but grow to way more than we can imagine!

When we say this prayer, we stop just asking for things we want for ourselves, and start finding out what God wants – for us and for the world.

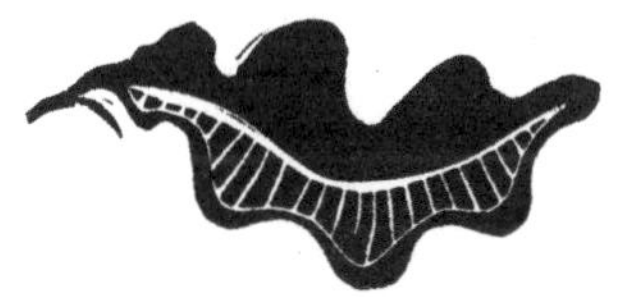

Thy will be done

God has a vision and a purpose for the world.

God loves peace and justice.

God wants us to love ourselves, to love each other and to love God.

God shows us how to do this by sending Jesus into the world.

God wants people to be free. God wants us to care for the earth and for each other.

Often, what we want is not what's best for us. Then, God weeps with us and for us when we fail, when things are wrong.

When we say this prayer, we seek what is best for everyone by seeking God's will for everything.

On earth as it is in heaven

God wants earth to be like heaven.

What this means is that all the good things that we see in God, God wants to see on earth.

God wants a world where we all enjoy being completely with God.

God wants a world where we love and respect each other.

God wants a world where we love and respect the earth itself.

God wants a world of peace.

When we say this prayer, we become part of God's movement of change, of bringing heaven down to earth.

Give us this day our daily bread

Jesus fed the hungry. He was a friend to everyone.
He cared for those who were in need.

Each of us needs food each day.

But there are lots of other things we need as well, like warmth, shelter, safety, comfort and love.

Some people in the world have these things.
Others don't.

Some people have so much food that they throw some of it away. Others have virtually nothing.

When we say this prayer, we are asking God that we may have what we need each day. We are also asking God to teach us not to want more than our share.

And forgive us our trespasses

Trespassing doesn't just mean straying onto someone else's property. It means doing things wrong.

Another word for 'trespass' is 'sin'. Sin is those things we know are wrong.

Most of us know what is wrong and what is right. From time to time, most of us feel guilty about the things we've done wrong.

We may not always say we are sorry. Even when we know we should.

We look at Jesus. We see how he loved and cared for everyone. We also see how he forgave people, even the people who nailed him to the cross.

God's forgiveness is there for each of us – we just have to accept it.

When we say this prayer, we are saying sorry for the things we've done wrong, and sorry for not doing the things we know we should have done. We are also thanking God that in Jesus we are all forgiven.

As we forgive those who trespass against us

This is the one bit of the Lord's Prayer that comes with a condition. If we want God to forgive us, we should be ready to forgive others.

This can be really hard.

There is a lot that's wrong in our lives. People hurt each other every day with the words they use and the choices they make. There is hurt in our families, in our schools and towns, and there are areas of enormous hurt when we look around the world, like hunger, pollution, conflict and war. Some people have so many things and others have so little.

If we pray, 'your kingdom come, your will be done', then we must be ready to forgive, and make amends. Our small choices can have a surprising impact on the bigger hurts of the world too. Like a little mustard seed growing into a huge tree.

When we say this prayer, we are saying that we are ready to live differently and ready to forgive those who hurt us, and that we want to build a different sort of world.

And lead us not into temptation

There are plenty of people who will tell you that forgiving others, not asking for more than your share, being sorry when you get things wrong, and trying to follow a way of life that is best for everyone is ridiculous.

'Look after number one,' they will say. 'Put yourself first.'

Jesus shows us a different way. It is the only hope for peace in our world.

Therefore, we ask God to save us when we are tempted to just live our own way and put ourselves first – and from all the other temptations that exist in the world.

When we say this prayer, we are asking God to be with us when things get difficult.

But deliver us from evil

There is evil in the world.

There is the wickedness people do to each other.

There is the darkness of life outside of God.

It is easy to turn away from God's way of life.

It is easy *not* to say the Lord's Prayer and *not* live the way God asks us.

It is easy to see Jesus and ignore him.
Or forget him.

But Jesus will never forget you. He is always there.

When we say this prayer, we are asking God to be with us even in the darkest times, when we see evil or when we forget God.

For thine is the kingdom, the power and the glory

We end the prayer looking away from us and back to God – 'God, everything is yours!'

All the good we long to see, all the bad we ask God to make better – we say again that God is King over all things.

When we say God has power, we don't simply mean God is a very, very powerful superhero. We are talking about the power of love, which is the greatest power in the universe and comes from God.

‘God is love,’ says the Bible, ‘and those who live in love live in God.’

This is the power that God has. It is also the glory. God is the greatest, most beautiful thing there is.

When we say this prayer, we are acknowledging that everything comes from God and everything belongs to God.

For ever and ever

The things God gives us in Jesus are for now.

They are also for eternity.

Jesus teaches us how to live our lives today.

By his cross and resurrection, Jesus shows us the future – our life with God for ever.

'I have come so that you can have life in all its fullness,' says Jesus.

When we say this prayer, we are asking God to be with us today to show us the way, and to be with us for ever.

Amen

The word Amen means 'I agree'.

We say it at the end of this prayer – and every prayer – to make it our own, to say we agree with it.

But do we?

This is the great challenge of THE LORD'S PRAYER. We say it, but do we mean it? It is by far the most said prayer in the world. It may also be the least meant.

Someone once said that if you could say
THE LORD'S PRAYER once and truly mean it,
you would be in heaven.

So let us keep trying. Let us persevere.
Let us say THE LORD'S PRAYER each day.

Let us say Amen to all it tells us.

When we say this prayer – especially the Amen at the end – we are saying we agree. We are trying to live and pray in the way Jesus gives us.

I dedicate this book to all those children and adults who long for heaven to be in earth. I thank God for those who taught me THE LORD'S PRAYER, but also for the many children whose comments and questions have been my best teacher down through the years. Thanks also to Ruth Roff and all the team at Hodder for making this book happen; and to Jack Seymour whose beautiful illustrations bring the book to life and invite us to wonder at it its meaning.

SC

Jack Seymour is an English teacher, graphic designer and illustrator – he's worked with various organisations including the British and Irish Lions, Land Rover, Google, Ordinance Survey and The Stewards' Trust as well as illustrating books and book covers. He works in lino, etching, monoprint, pen & ink and watercolour.

Author of many books for children and adults, Stephen Cottrell is the Archbishop of York, one of the most senior posts in the Church of England. However, his life's work as a priest as well as a bishop has been to tell the story of the Christian faith in ways that are simple, compelling and lovely. This little book is just one more way of explaining and telling that story. When he isn't 'bishoping', Stephen loves to walk, cook, eat and write. He also makes lino prints, though not nearly as good as Jack's, though somehow one managed to sneak its way into this book! Stephen is married to Rebecca, who is a potter. They have three sons, two grandchildren and one dog, Molly.